No Brother, This Storm

For those of us from the swamps and coastal marshes, a Jack Bedell poem often says what we feel but could not say. His ability to focus his eye on the landscape and deftly place us among the reeds is an uncommon gift, but one we have come to take for granted in his work. The poems in *No Brother, This Storm* are stark in their vision and deep in their wisdom. We devour these poems the way the water devours land, and we ready our bones for flight.

—J. Bruce Fuller, author of
The Dissenter's Ground and *Flood*

With the acute perceptions of a seasoned poet, Jack Bedell's *No Brother, This Storm* speaks poignantly of what we love—how place and family prevail over what passes away. Attentive to the world around him, the Cajun and coastal Louisiana of his youth and current life, family history, and folklore are impressively interwoven, traversing generations "to mingle with our dreams / for as long as the river flows." The range of these poems is no narrow playing field; each poem resonates with the wider world, engaging us through the humanity we all share. Storms take their toll when "blacktopped roads lead nowhere", and uncertain sounds in a swamp mean following an omen "like compass needles" to safety. Grace comes when a "Cold morning becomes psalm", when "there is no other shelter to offer /.../save/ color and soft voices." It is through such images, compelling and rich, that Bedell's poems draw resilience from what blesses our lives, rendering *No Brother, This Storm* a luminous, exemplary work.

—Jeffrey Alfier, editor of Blue Horse Press
and *San Pedro River Review*

No Brother, This Storm takes us on a stroll into the humid, fecund waterways of Jack Bedell's portion of the Gulf Coast called Louisiana. But don't be fooled into thinking that this gorgeously rendered landscape is anything less than the dreamscape that haunts us all—the internal externalized into tableaus full of those who have come before and those to whom we seek to give the future as a holy present. The greatest gift (and there are many) of this sequence of poems is that through their careful, painterly, and meditative aspects we ourselves become "revenant," that is, Bedell's walk with us transforms us into someone who returns as transparent with meaning and hopeful beauty as are his poems.

—Sarah Cortez, author of *Cold Blue Steel*

It's the tender urgencies that get me every time in Jack Bedell's poems. These *No Brother, This Storm* poems lean into eternal return: a father saving things against themselves, uncles whose enigmatic sayings are finally realized, dosgris diving for food, a dead turtle's last stretch into grace, the pelican's fight into the wind, ancient timeless wind in hair, and that part of the place making the sea grass green. Each poem here is as alive as yeast in sweet dough rising in a mother's kitchen.

—Darrell Bourque, former Louisiana Poet Laureate
and author of *Megan's Guitar and Other Poems
from Acadie* and *Where I Waited*

No Brother, This Storm

Jack B. Bedell

MERCER UNIVERSITY PRESS | *Macon, Georgia*
2018

MUP/ P572

Published by Mercer University Press
1501 Mercer University Drive
Macon, Georgia 31207

9 8 7 6 5 4 3 2 1

Books published by Mercer University Press are printed on acid-free paper
that meets the requirements of the American National Standard for
Information Sciences—Permanence of Paper for Printed Library Materials.

Printed and bound in CANADA.

This book is set in Adobe Caslon.

ISBN   978-0-88146-675-1
Cataloging-in-Publication Data is available from the Library of Congress

Contents

MERCER UNIVERSITY PRESS

Endowed by

TOM WATSON BROWN
and
THE WATSON-BROWN FOUNDATION, INC.

Acknowledgments

Special thanks to the editors of the following publications in which some of these poems originally appeared:

"Coastal, Aberration," *About Place*; "Tabulation," *Dialogist*; "Elliptic," "Barometric," "Shift, Dunes," and "Breakwater," *The Fourth River*; "Autance," *Gnarled Oak*; "Coda" and "*Les Ris*," *Hoot*; "First Kiss," *Hudson Review*; "Frissons," *The Journal of Compressed Creative Arts*; "Des Exiles Acadiens dans le Port du Boston," 1755" and "Wellfire," *Louisiana Cultural Vistas*; "Remnant," *MockingHeart Review*; "Dark Current," "Pere Papineau," and " A Trick of Light," *Peacock Journal*; "Hyperlapse," "*Prédire*," and "Marsh," *Poetry South*; "Parabolic," *River Teeth*; "16 Lines for Her Voice," *San Pedro River Reiveiw*; "Morning, Vigil" and "Storm, Grand Isle," *Southern Quarterly*; "Lutins," *Split Rock Review*; "Smoke, Mirror," *Sport Literate*; "Dead Turtle" and "Just a Beginning," *The Swamp*; "The Argument from Patience" and "*Revenant*," *Town Creek Poetry*; "Souvenir du Printemps," *Windhover: A Journal of Christian Literature*.

The following poems were included in anthologies:

"First Kiss." *33*. Negative Capability Press; "El Tajin" and "On Days Like This, Undone," *Goodbye, Mexico: Poems of Remembrance*, Texas Review Press, 2015; "Caernavon, Mississippi River Flood, 1927" and "Like from the Tip of a Staff," *Down to the Dark River: Contemporary Poems about the Mississippi River*, Louisiana Literature Press, 2016; "Elliptic," *Southern Ecology: An Anthology of Literature and the Environment*, Yellow Flag Press, 2017.

Additionally, many of these poems appeared in the limited edition chapbooks *Elliptic* (Yellow Flag Press, 2016) and *Revenant* (Blue Horse Press, 2016).

I.

THERE AND THAT

Remnant

They happen in the kitchen, these visits
with my mother. She's always working, something
busy, like separating yolks for chix buns.

Alive, she would've passed the eggs through her fingers,
letting the whites drip through, holding the yolks
gently in her palm. During these dreams, though,

she uses the shells like they do on cooking shows
passing the yolks from half to half before
dropping them into the mixing bowl. She makes

her dough patiently, without much fuss,
pressing it out and balling it up quietly
in the hollow of an old balsa plank.

When the dough is gold and dense enough,
she raises the plank as high as she can
above her head to place it in the warm spot

on top of the refrigerator. Straining like this
she is so much like herself I can barely breathe.
If I try to help her or open my mouth to speak,

the alarm will go off and morning will burn itself
onto the day. Quiet or not, I can never stay
long enough for the dough to rise, for her

to roll and cut the buns, place them in the oven
on buttered sheets. Even though I'll wake
before the smell hits me, the taste remains.

Revenant

On the Pass at Manchac
a camp has toppled from its pilings.
Its porch frowns down into the lake.

My son studies weather patterns
for class. His book claims
the wind circulating around us
is the same wind that stirred the sand
around Giza while men were building
pyramids, that swayed the lilies
of the valley and filled sails toward Vinland.

I imagine God sighing into clay
to give it life. Years later that breath
swirls into a storm off Africa,
dances for weeks across the Atlantic
into the Gulf and onto our shore
to nudge a camp off its perch
on the Point, the one place
my mother loved on her drive
back home, always rolling her window down
to feel a breeze in her hair.

First Kiss

I cannot keep my daughter's mind
off baby frogs. My father caught one
for her the other day and put it
in the hollow of her palm. She fell
for its smooth green skin and shiny eyes,
loved how it held her fingertips
in its tiny hands. Now she's a huntress.

As soon as the coffee pot goes off
in the morning, she's dressed
and staring out the back-door glass,
waits on point until I release the bolt,
setting her to motion. There's no
distracting her with linguistics, the difference
between *crapaud* and *ouaouaron*. She wants

to turn over every pot, pull back
the cover on the barbecue pit,
check each slat in the storm shutters.
She knows no crack is too small
for these frogs. They can flatten themselves
and get under anything. They fold their bones
and wait for her, each one a prince.

Morning, Vigil

My uncle knew nothing still
wants to be moved.
He'd captained boats most of his life,

learned this pushing barges
around the intracoastal canal
by moonlight. It's why

he'd walk five blocks to St. Bernadette
in total darkness to wake the priests
for weekday mass, why he'd stand

or kneel, but never sit
for services, every part of him
flowing and vigilant.

Parabolic

His first summer married, my father tended
chickens. His job was to chase the birds
out of the tin coop on hot days. They piled
on top of each other in the corner of the shed
no matter how hot it got in there.

He had to fight his way through their bodies
until he reached the back wall. Unless
he could tease the deepest chickens in the coop
to shuffle back out into the sunlight,
none of the other birds would leave.

Whenever he grabbed the ones pressed against the wall
and threw them towards the door, they'd run
back to press themselves into the flock again.
The only way to save the birds was to make them
choose the outside air for themselves.

If he couldn't, the whole dirt floor would be piled
white with dead feathers, too many bodies even
for the workers to carry home to their wives for supper.

Tabulation

What my father knew
he could calculate

with small pad
and pencil nub,
                        factor
length of pipe
and drilling angle

through soft soil
or through rock.
                        No matter
if he lost a finger to metal coupling
or burned in an explosion,

nothing would change
how numbers fit
together on his page—
neatly in lines
like children on a dock's edge,
               waving.

Transposition

My son cannot find
a path to pass through

the math on his page,
cannot balance

left to right.
He loses his hold

on whatever variables
float inside the syntax

of the problems he faces,
bites down on his molars

hard enough to stress
the enamel. There's nothing

I can do to help him,
except fear the fractures
we cannot see, imagine
a proof somewhere

of something.

Summer, Cottonmouth

—for Emma

Cut in a half-dozen pieces
in the scoop of a shovel,
the moccasin was not dead to my daughter,

not scales and blood,
nor fangs loosed
below milky eyes.

Its life still huddled
into narrative for her,
even as its headless muscles writhed.

Shift, Dunes

Three hills down under rolling clouds
my son tracks sand crabs
by long, curving lines they cut

across the dunes. Waves burst onto the shore
near his feet. Gulls float overhead
tracking his movement

as he disappears into a gully
between hills.
                   It would be difficult

not to fret, to ignore
the absence of his bright
shirt billowing in gusts,

not to wonder
what fat jellyfish
he might scoop into his net,
what sharp mess
may have washed ashore
to find his bare soles.

                 Difficult,
if not for the gulls' persistence.

Hyperlapse

Driving west of Lafayette
    I catch the AM feed
        from Fred's Lounge in Mamou.

As soon as the static clears,
    the house band fires up "'tit Galop."
        A sound that's lingered

in me for years pierces the mic.
    Like the slide of my mother's house shoes
        on kitchen tile or the rising fuss

of a wet baby, the triangle's shuffle
    moves me in time, presses the back
        of a woman whose name I can't speak

straight into the center of my palm,
    and my feet begin
        to misremember the floor.

On Days Like This, Undone

—for my wife, 12.24.2014

On days like this with shopping left to do,
or tomorrow with meals to make
and mess to undo, or any of those that follow
with homework to strafe through and needs
piling up at your feet, days when we pass
in the hallway getting ready our separate lists,
or pass each other on the road carting kids
to practices on opposite sides of town,
this is the peace I wish for you—

Your toes spreading in the sand.
Your beach chair tilted into the sun.
I hear sunsets are lovely off Manzanillo
year around, so there and that, for sure,
with fish seared just right on both sides,
served with tortillas fresh from someone else's work.
So don't move, wife, the Pacific will whisper.
Rest your feet. Let the breeze stir
this sand, confectionary. The beer
is already within reach, almost
        too cold to drink.

Les Ris

Sweet roll dough,
yellow with yolk,

waits in the warm spot
on top of the fridge.
It swells under a kitchen towel,

alive and becoming
the reason Sundays glow,

promises we roll
and cut, bake and glaze,
share with lips already parted,
smiling.

A Wedding, In Rain

It's good luck, the rain, my wife says
to the stranger behind us.

If I was any luckier, the man smiles back,
they'd put me in jail, then.

And the young preacher starts
talking about hard times and how

people are worse more than they are
better. And the young couple

cares nothing about sermons
or luck or how the raindrops

fall straight through the giant oak
reaching out over their heads.

They just hold hands and look
into each other's eyes, see

the person they know is right
there with them, not the flawed

sinner the young preacher keeps
telling them they'll wake up to

tomorrow. And the old people
daubing rain off their glasses

know the walk back up
to the reception hall won't be

nearly as kind, uphill and slick
after this little blessing of luck.

But for right now, there's song
and prayer and promises,

more than two people
happy to be here, wet.

Dead Turtle

My daughter leaves the body
as it lies, will not disturb
the turtle's last stretch
to position it with more grace.

She covers it with azalea petals
to cool its skin, outlines
its body in concentric circles
of branches, swatches
torn from magazines—

there is no other shelter to offer
from the sun or ants, save
color and soft voices.

In some other place, she will find
song to hold all of this, enlaced.

II.

GONE TO GULF

Dark Current

Stranded in our yard
    by backwash of river
        and a foot of rain,

a snapping turtle rolls
    on its shell, perpetual
        as if fallen in a dream.

Its claws cannot find river bottom
    for purchase, and nothing
        in the sea foam of leaves

gathering around its body
    can satisfy its chomping jaws.
        No wind to carry it

where it must go, no light
    bright enough to dry this mess,
        no brother, this storm.

A Trick of Light

I thought I saw a chinchilla
    escaped from my uncle's cages
        dart across our backyard—

silver against dead grass,
    fat, unable to move
        in straight lines.

It could easily have been worry
    scurrying between bare spots
        in the sod, drawing

attention to work undone,
    to promises I've failed to keep.
        Could've been fear

scuttling from tuition bills
    to poor decisions
        left strewn about the yard,

unkempt. Of course,
    it could have been bad light,
        or nothing much at all.

Elliptic

—Bayou Sauvage

Lines of reeds where land
releases to the Gulf, back wash
into salt and wave—

                          if we were to lay our dead
here to guard this shore
against new storms,

                          we could not
pile bones quickly enough
to outpace this loss,

                          would never
stave off such constant

         leaving.

Barometric

Wind built in the trees
     as my uncle fought
         knots of rope

to tie down the crab traps
     stacked behind our camp.

Whatever was ours
     not already taken
         by the Gulf

had to be bound to ground,
     away from the surge and swell

bearing down on our land.
     Gray sky circled overhead and fear
         became a luxury. Every second

wasted with mistake turned to anger,
     shone like a bonfire calling the storm.
         Soon, we would cook a meal to welcome her home.

Storm, Grand Isle

The surf stretches
      thigh-deep to the horizon.

Campless pilings creak
      against the mounting waves,

their moans haunting the island
      much more than the seabirds overhead.

All the way from the Caribbean,
      new winds climb on shore.

Barren since the horn sounded,
      blacktopped roads lead nowhere.

Breakwater

It is not recovery: no way to lure coastline
        back into place, recall silt
                already gone to Gulf.

More like conception,
        as helicopters
                lift piles of Christmas trees

into air, drop them
        in bundles along the marsh line.
                Reeds will grow

in soil trapped here.
        Shrimp will hide
                as these ponds fill in,

ducks will land in flocks
        to feed. All new gifts
                against the water's need.

Prédire

Just below the tree line
      clouds congeal
            out of view.

Winds shift course
      enough to bend tall grass,
            clean smell of water on air.

Cattle lie sloe-eyed
      in tight clusters
            along the north fence.

The old women see them
      go to ground
            and know.

Frissons

Sometimes a *yawp* comes
      from the marsh.

It echoes over the trees
      and stirs

turtles from their posts
      atop cypress logs.

Do not look for a bruise
      in the sky

or some vacuum of light
      sucking from that direction.

The hair will rise
      a certain way

on the back of your neck
      and forearms.

Follow these omens
      like compass needles

leading you some other,
      any other, place.

Marsh

I cannot think of another place
as part of me—

reeds and water to the horizon line,
space and game to live,

fish for stew, turtles for sauce picante,
bullfrogs and moonlight for deep sleep.

A place of practiced rules,
heavy pull, lessons

passed down, preserved
like strawberry jam

put on the shelf for cold mornings
when herons take flight in fog.

Acutance

Pull in the nets,
swollen from seven passes off the Gulf.

White boots squeak on wet deck,
knots loosen and shrimp slide
out of twine, onto wood.

What rolled underfoot
now buzzes with shell and fin.

Sorting bins fill with overs and unders.
Lemon fish are swept into the hold for bait.

Stingrays flop to the sides
and are shoveled over,
reminders that days could be worse.

Just a Beginning

—for Julia Sims

Water ripples, and rustling
in the tops of trees
where herons
ready their bones for flight.

The photographer
coasts her boat toward
the middle of the lake.

Dawn bursts purple over Manchac.

Cold morning becomes psalm.

Off Bayou DuLarge

The *trainasse* where my uncle left me
        cut a straight line to the blind,
                an easy pass through high marsh.

Overhead, pintails circled
        in formation, looking
                for feed and other flocks.

I'd put the decoys out on the water
        and set up behind the reeds of the blind
                to start my calls. Short tick-a-ticks

to bring the ducks in for feeding,
        staccato pleas not even the sun
                could resist as it grew into the sky.

The Argument from Patience

The stillness of the lake when a dos-gris dives
spreads in all directions. The water's surface
      flattens into pure reflection, sky

stretches away from the tops of trees,
herons tuck their beaks underwing, and I wait.
      I scan from reeds to horizon,

and wait. I hold my breath, squint
into the setting light for anything
      to break into the air, with nothing

to do but wait. I know the bird's not gone.
It's just not here. I know it will come back
      when its belly fills, maybe thirty yards

down the bank, but still here. This place
will find movement again. All waiting
      must come to an end.

Coastal, Aberration

The packing shed and fishermen's homes swell
      in the background, cement and metal against gray sky.

Windows and skylights, even a single church cross,
     reach into the clouds. No work crew in sight.

The men inside must be waiting for weather to pass,
    or for the day boat to pull in

with bushels of fish to carry in from the dock,
     ice down for the trip to town,

dreaming of it.

       *

    In the foreground, three boats have found their final landing tied to
each other against the riprap. One vessel's sound, but broken up along its
gunwale, another with sturdy bow but torn in half behind its steering
wheel, the third just ribs with enough planks to separate it from the dirt.
The ships are bound together like a monument to work done and over,
time passed, never to come around again.

       *

Lichen and rust,
      boat ribs crumbling back to ground—

From earth   to axe   to sea   to shore

and dust.

       *

Between, rows of fish traps stacked
    against the wind's bite.
Green nets and yards of twine

readied for a storm.

*

On wing halfway above the horizon, a pelican fights into the wind.
Black and white against the gray, the bird's an aberration, wings pulsing,
a shift in tone between squall lines. Maybe it's a harbinger. Maybe a
scourge. Maybe, more than the traps, it's proof the sea cannot run barren.
Life is not decay, not the slow loss of color and grain. The bird will dive
into the surf soon enough, scoop up fish for its young, and carry that
catch back to its nest to spark a scene more vibrant than shored boats and
empty traps. Even in still photos, the narrative must flow.

*

Stones cover the shoreline, underfoot,
     becoming something other
     than what they are,
smaller, more part of the place,
     making the sea grass green.

III.

FABLES

Raconte

Whenever anything I cared about
    went missing, my mother
        told me the story of bears

who struggled every day
    to find the things
        they needed. They had no home

and moved around without rest
    under moonlight.
        She said they could cover

hundreds of miles before
    sunrise. There was never
        any logic to the things

the bears took, mother told me.
    Even they didn't know
        what sparkly thing,

or noise maker,
    or special picture book
        they had to have

until they held it
    in their huge paws,
        caught its shine in their eyes.

Traiteur

A stack of silver coins,
water from the church well
carried in an old wash basin,
rosary beads, unstrung
in a leather pouch; he prays
so soft in French the words
evaporate into the dark room
where the child he treats has held
a fever for two weeks, cannot
wake from violent dreams, legs
pumping under quilts.
He whispers a song over the boy,
takes the coins in his fist,
and jingles them just over
the child's skin from scalp
to toes. Does the same with the beads,
singing the whole while.
We hold the basin for him
as he sinks the boy's palms
then feet into the cool water
and bids us to leave the basin
under the bed, beneath the child's heart.
He spreads so much calm in the room
we have no words to thank him,
nothing he would ever accept.

Fable, *Un Matin*

As soon as the eyes and snout showed up
floating in his cattle pond one morning,
the farmer began to count the stock

roaming his fields. He'd never taken
inventory before, but thought
his numbers smaller than they ought to be.

He set about watching the alligator
swim around his pond that day,
knowing it wouldn't leave as quickly

as it had appeared. He'd told his children
bedtime stories of wise gators
who'd outwitted raccoons and bullfrogs,

read in wildlife books how long
it took for them to grow past fifteen feet,
how gentle and patient they were

courting love, always circling
and waiting, slapping their broad throats
on the water's surface for attention.

But fables could not save his calves
nosing grass at the water's edge,
nor spare the white chickens pecking

head down along the bank. His ledger
was not difficult to balance.
He had no meat to lose heading

towards winter and plenty 12-gauge shells
back at the house, the walk too short
to break much of a sweat.

Souvenir du Printemps

On his way to work, the father leaves his son
at the levee to count the persistence of woodpeckers
knocking in the tops of pine trees.
                                    The father's day
fills with well pressures, fishing tools,
men who cannot find wet in the rain.
The son's with snakes at the water's edge
and sugar cane to chew.
                                    Welders' dogs
scurry through the days of both, barking
where there should be quiet, quiet when
the men step outside for smokes.
                                    Field mice
wait inside the reeds for the sun to drop,
the father for all his pipe to come out of the ground
fully sound and ready for tomorrow,
                                    the boy
for supper when chairs fill and all hands join
in prayer, a meal set out for the taking.

Wellfire

The hospital's grey cinderblock
      a frame for the line of men
sitting along the banquette.
      Beneath a canopy of smoke,
the tips of their Pall Malls
      dance like fireflies in the dark.
The men's faces obscured
      but surely there, singed
and blistered, hold
      discomfort and relief in the corners
of their eyes. This one time
      the sequence broke their way,
facts blunt as fire—
      gas pumps shutting down,
magnetos turning one too many times,
      sparks releasing into fumes.
Those too slow to feel it coming
      are home with family now.
Those quick to run towards trouble
      were blown to the ceiling,
skin fried, hair burned off,
      onyx melted out of their masonic rings.
Stuck here queued up for salve
      and bandages, they bum cigarettes
from each other, knowing
      full well the waiting line
won't be this long next time.

Smoke, Mirror

"When a man gets in your blood like that, you can't never let go."
—Joe Frazier

A half dozen people have told me
they'd die for me, would give
their lives for my love.
Every one of them is still alive,
in some other town, raising
someone else's children.

When I was nine, I watched Joe Frazier
try his best to die for me in Manila.
My father let me stay home from school
to wait in line for the cable box to watch the fight.
We were together all day, waiting.

I don't remember eating
or talking at all that day,
just the explosion of hate
released by the opening bell.

Half-blind to start and all blind
by the third round, Frazier planted
his forehead in Ali's chest, followed
the man's breath around the huge ring,
walking through fists like rain.

By the fifth, Frazier had Ali
off his toes and cringing.
To him, Ali was a sack of bricks
hung over a tree limb in South Carolina,
and he punished that dead weight
for its uselessness. My father and I
threw every punch with him
and prayed for the one
that would put Ali to ground.

We watched Frazier catch rights
until his face opened and his eyes shut.
Watched him shuffle forward into darkness
round after round. What he wanted
was plain to see. We wanted it, too.
What kept him standing and chasing
and throwing hands outdistanced
even that desire.

In the fourteenth, Frazier took
nine straight shots to the head
without landing anything himself,
and I thought for a second
he was dead on his feet,
but he closed out the round
digging into Ali's body, taking
what soul the man had to give.
One more punch would have ended it,
both ways.

Then it was over. The men
in Frazier's corner valued life
with a different economy
than he did, saw tomorrow
as better currency than a fifteenth round.
They did not see Ali in his own corner
slumped and ready for it to end.
Only that it had to end.

There's no forgetting how Frazier
jumped off his stool, begging
through the blood in his mouth
for one more punch, one more
lunge into the darkness.
I saw how far he was willing to go
and will always love him for it.

El Tajin

The rules of this place announce themselves
on the stones surrounding the ball court.
Every wall holds stories of players
who travailed here in front of parents,
wives, neighbors, kings. Even gods
lounged in vats of pulque on the hillsides
watching these warriors run the field.

Their game was brutally simple—
keep a rubber ball off the ground
without hands or feet, find
space on a surface long and slender
like a serpent's back, beat
the other men with speed and desire.
Do these things and heaven opens.

The carvings show all this
in glorious tribute. They also preserve
the history of warriors who failed,
their hands held behind their backs,
their necks tilted toward the setting sun,
the knife poised close to open
its own path to heaven.

It's easy to imagine parents shining
with pride in this dying light. From above
the north court, I could see my own son
running free as he does on a soccer field
every weekend, taller and faster than the others.
His would be a fine head to offer
these gods, hair golden, eyes blazing blue.

16 Lines for Her Voice

—after Ms. Jenavieve Cook

On the bar's stoop:
>banjo and percussive bass,
>>clarinet and trumpet syncopate

in ragtime groove
>while two pit bulls deadpan stare.

Plenty enough sound
>to stop the banquette crowd
>>up Frenchman Street

until she swaps her trumpet
>for megaphone and we're all
>>drawn into a Victrola's horn

spinning time upstream
>a century ago. Rasp

and tremolo on the backside
>of her breath bring now
>>to its knees.

Like from the Tip of a Staff

—Jim Bowie off Natchez, Mississippi, 1827

The Mississippi has always made
        its choices. Since Paul Bunyan

dragged his axe in Minnesota
        and scored its course,

the river has fed some land,
        starved some, climbed its banks

to fill deltas. It's sunken barges,
        floated men to riches,

sucked others down into silt,
        or, like Jim Bowie,

carried the blood they've spilled
        into history, east up the Ohio,

toward the Pacific in the Missouri,
        over spillways through the Atchafalaya.

Shot in the hip, stabbed and cut
        after a duel that wasn't his,

all Bowie had to do was bleed
        into the river for his name to mean

something to us all, for the knife
        his brother honed for him to stick

in our memories, its blade curved
        and meandering as the river itself.

Like from the tip of a staff, Bowie's blood
  dripped into the Mississippi

to mingle with our dreams
  for as long as the river flows.

Caernavon, Mississippi River Flood, 1927

After they blew the levee with dynamite,
the river came for a visit, simple as that.
Like some cypress witch, it crept out from the trees
one night, right up to the porch steps,
brought mud, dead wood, egrets pecking around
with so little meat on their bones they'd barely bleed
when the bullet passed through, and horse flies
so big and fierce they'd have given Job pause.

For weeks the water lapped against the house,
made sway and a little breeze. April clouds
rolled across the sky but spared us rain.
Spared New Orleans, too, with all the water
dammed in St. Bernard. But as witches are wont to do
the water disappeared under moonlight in May,
taking any goodness it had brought with it,
leaving stillness, heat, and rotten silt.

Without the sheen of moon on the water,
the slow rock of waves against the house's stilts,
our lives succumbed to gravity. Inside and out
there was cleaning to do, and things to make
right. Too many things, though, were breached
forever. All our animals were washed away,
all the grass they'd eat was dead. Even our love
had followed that witch past the farthest tree.

Des Exilés Acadiens dans le Port du Boston, 1755

Tie the boat to the dock,
one loose loop in case

you are turned back at port.
As the oldest boy stamps out

the bow light, the girls collect
what food is left. Wife

holds baby to her chest,
rocking with the tide, offering

her fingers to the crying mouth.
Down the dock, moonlight

pulses, other families disembark
toward shorefront windows

lighting one by one,
not nearly as welcoming in day
as they appear this night.

Père Papineau

—an Acadian folk tale

I.

The old man should not be met
       at water's edge.

He will come inland,
       follow you back home

hungry.

Always leave him to his thoughts,
       the heron's cry.

II.

Wanderer   no bog or hollow
the old man hasn't crossed.

His hunger pulls him around,
bottomless, ready to consume a man's weight.

Never try to feed his demands
or give him reason to cast spells.

There's not enough rice in the field,
nor chickens in the coop,

to fill the hole in his gut.
Do not confuse his wanting with need.

III.

The nature of the marsh
is to take things in,
interlace water and reed,
heat and sound,
stranger and friend.

The old man, though,
is dos-gris,
and we are all mullet
in his world.

Lutins

Today, walking the neighborhood,
I ran across a white cat.

It did not stop for me,
but stared me down

as if I'd offended it
somehow.

Cats always worried
my uncle's camp when I was young.

Even though he kept chinchillas
out back, he trusted the cats

to clean the dock
after he'd baited crab traps.

Not the white ones, though.
He ran those off,

said cats without color
were *lutins*. They turned

to goblins in moonlight,
troubled the horses so much

the animals couldn't walk
rice fields in the mornings.

Lutins rode the horses' backs
until dawn, plaited

their tails and manes
to let the farmers know

who owned the fields
first. No keyhole was ever

small enough to keep *lutins* out
if they wanted in.

My uncle always said
he was happy to have

more horses than hair.
Can't say I ever understood that

until now.

Coda

Afternoons beside the spillway,
old men cast lines into the water

and stare at their corks,
waiting still for the channel cat

that stole their bait decades ago
to pull itself out of the silt,

rise giant and hungry
toward the last hook they have.

About the Author

Jack B. Bedell is Professor of English and Coordinator of Creative Writing at Southeastern Louisiana University where he also edits *Louisiana Literature* and directs the Louisiana Literature Press. His latest collections are *Revenant* (Blue Horse Press, 2016), *Elliptic* (Yellow Flag Press, 2016), and *Bone-Hollow, True: New & Selected Poems, Call & Response, Come Rain, Come Shine, What Passes for Love* and *At the Bonehouse*, all published by Texas Review Press (a member of the Texas A&M Press Consortium). His work has appeared in the *Southern Review, Sport Literate, The Fourth River, Hudson Review, Connecticut Review, Paterson Literary Review, Texas Review, Southern Quarterly,* and other journals. Bedell is the recipient of the Louisiana Endowment for the Humanities Individual Achievement in the Humanities Award and the Governor's Award for Artistic Achievement, and he is currently serving as Louisiana Poet Laureate, 2017–2019. He and his wife Beth have three children, Jack, Jr., Samuel Eli, and Emma Louise.